About This Book

Title: *Ears Can Hear*

Step: 6

Word Count: 246

Skills in Focus: Long vowel-r combinations

Tricky Words: between, body, auricle, canal, vibrates, infection, through

Ideas For Using This Book

Before Reading:
- **Comprehension:** Look at the title and cover image together. Walk through the pictures in the book with readers and have them make predictions about what they might learn while reading.
- **Accuracy:** Practice saying the tricky words listed on page 1.
- **Phonics:** Tell students they will read words with long vowel-r combinations. Explain that for some vowel-r combinations, such as *-air* and *-eer*, the word keeps its long vowel sound. Next, explain that the spelling combination *-ear* can be pronounced in different ways: /uhr/ as in *learn*, /air/ as in *bear*, and /eer/ as in *hear*. Have students look at the word *hear* in the title on the front cover. Ask readers to point to the letters that make the sound /eer/. Write this word on a piece of paper, underlining the letters that represent the target sound. Repeat with the story words *your*, *ear*, *cheer*, and *air*.

During Reading:
- Have readers point under each word as they read it.
- **Decoding:** If readers are stuck on a word, help them say each sound and blend the sounds together smoothly. Be sure to point out words with long vowel-r combinations as they appear.
- **Comprehension:** Invite readers to talk about new things they are learning about ears and hearing while reading. What are they learning that they didn't know before?

After Reading:
Discuss the book. Some ideas for questions:
- What are some sounds that you hear every day?
- What do you still wonder about ears and hearing?

Ears Can Hear

Text by Laura Stickney

Reading Consultant
Deborah MacPhee, PhD
Professor, School of Teaching and Learning
Illinois State University

PICTURE WINDOW BOOKS
a capstone imprint

Your ears are
on your head.

You have one ear on
each side of your
head, near your hair.

Ears are organs, or body parts with a job. These organs are for hearing.

They help you hear sounds.

Your ear has three parts. These are the outer ear, middle ear, and inner ear.

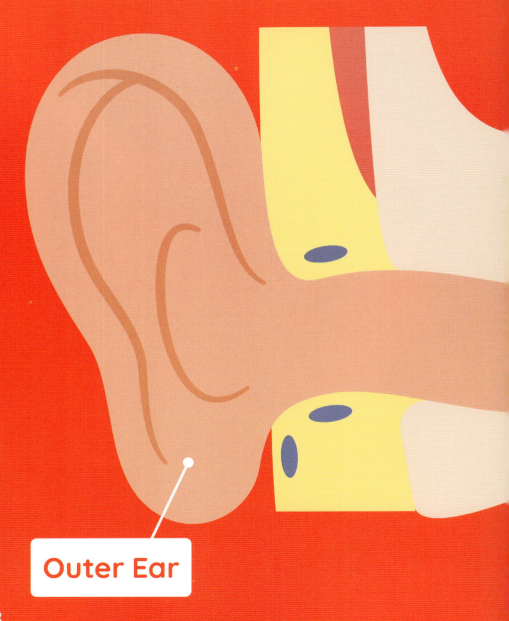

Outer Ear

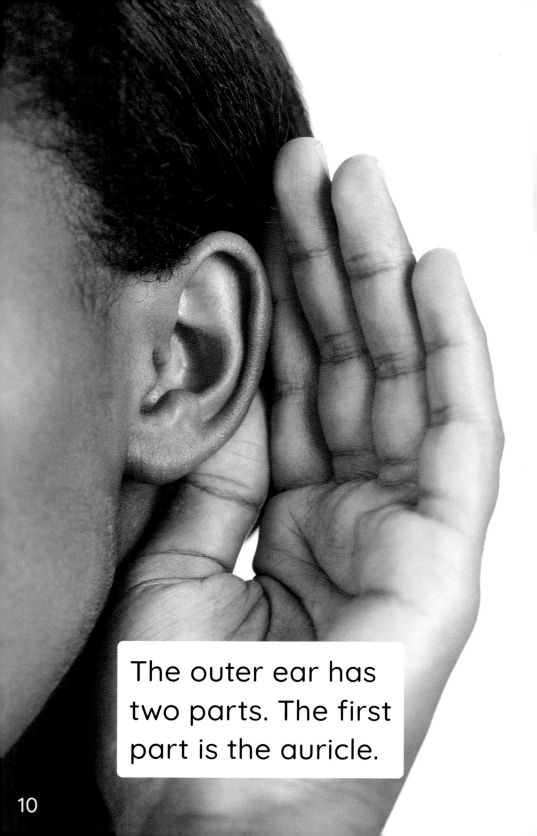

The outer ear has two parts. The first part is the auricle.

Your earlobe is part of the auricle.

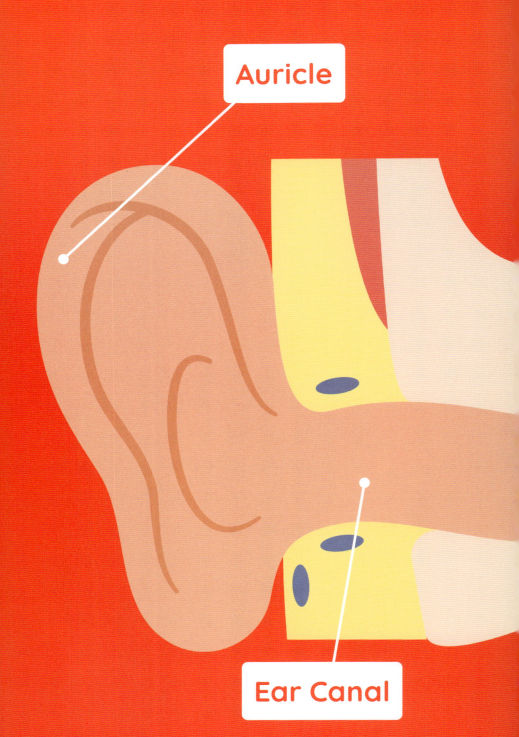

Between your middle ear and outer ear is an eardrum.

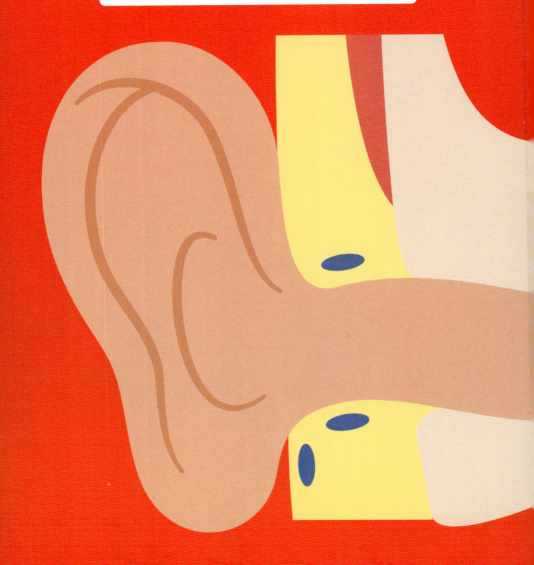

Sound waves bounce off your eardrum. The eardrum vibrates. It sends sounds to the inner ear.

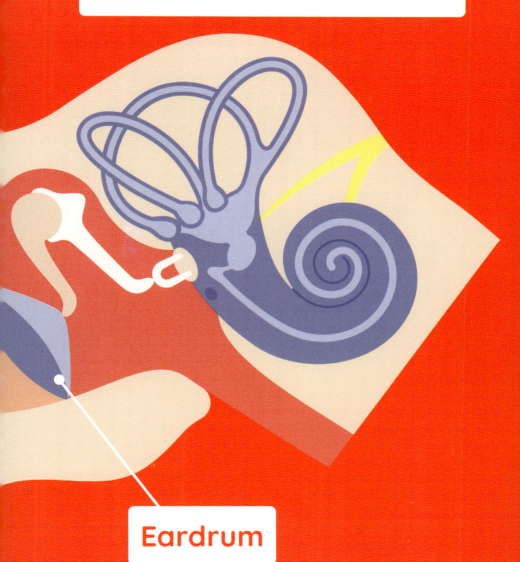

Eardrum

The inner ear has coiled organs. The organs pick up the sound waves.

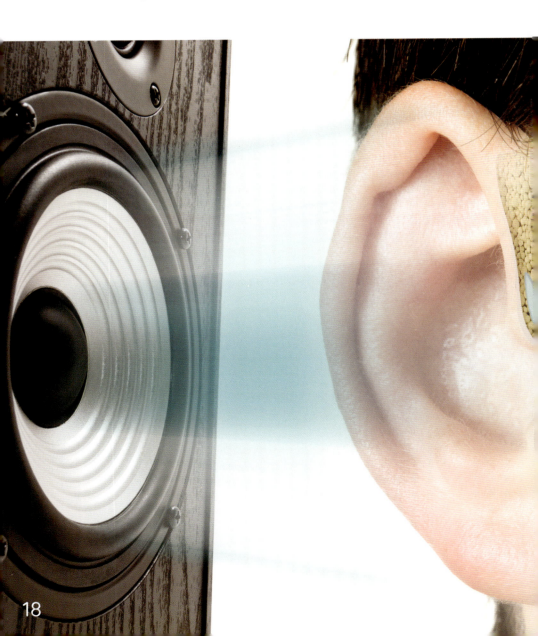

Their job is to send sounds to your brain.

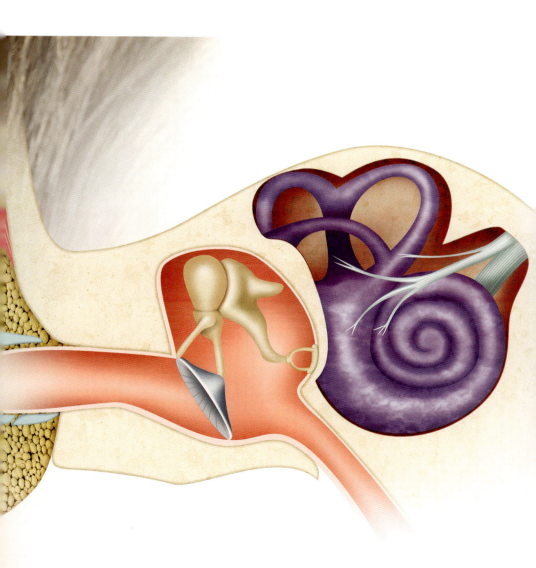

Ears can hear loud sounds. They can hear doors slam.

They can hear horses snort.

Ears can hear soft sounds. They can hear whispers.

Ears can hear deer creep across the forest floor.

When you fly in a plane, your ears are high in the air.

This can make your ears pop.

You must care for your ears. Keep them clean.

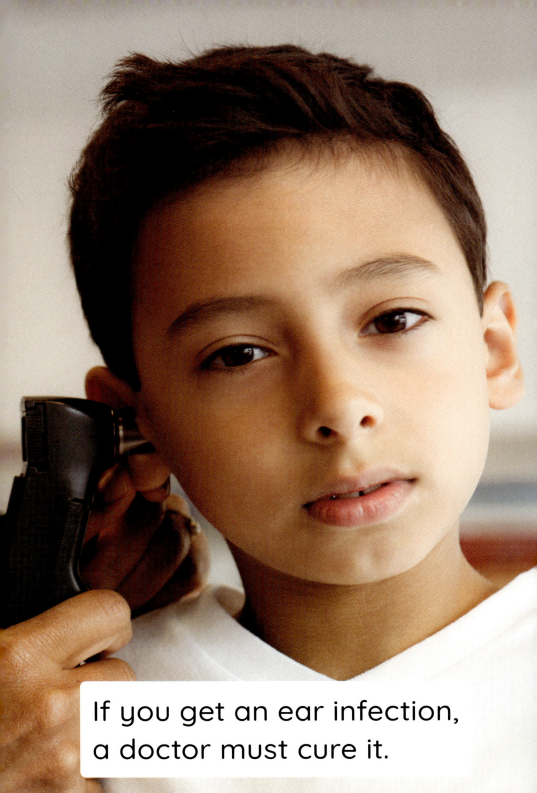

If you get an ear infection, a doctor must cure it.

What sounds can you hear with your ears?

More Ideas:

Phonics Activity

Writing with Long Vowel-r Combinations:
Ask readers to write a story using as many words as possible that have long vowel-r combinations. The story can be as silly or serious as readers want!

Suggested words: hear, ear, your, air, deer, cheer

Extended Learning Activity

Listen Up:
Ask readers to spend a few minutes listening to the sounds around them. Then ask them to try making their own sounds. Have readers write a list of the different sounds they heard and made. Have them write a few sentences about the sounds. Were the sounds loud or soft? Challenge students to use words with long vowel-r combinations in their sentences.

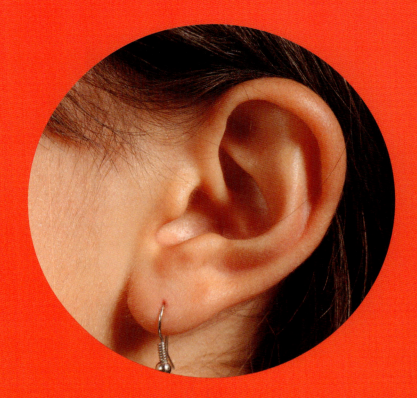

Published by Picture Window Books, an imprint of Capstone
1710 Roe Crest Drive, North Mankato, Minnesota 56003
capstonepub.com

Copyright © 2026 by Capstone.
All rights reserved. No part of this publication may be reproduced in whole or in part, or stored in a retrieval system, or transmitted in any form or by any means, electronic, mechanical, photocopying, recording, or otherwise, without written permission of the publisher.

Library of Congress Cataloging-in-Publication Data is available on the Library of Congress website.

ISBN: 9798875227264 (hardback)
ISBN: 9798875231414 (paperback)
ISBN: 9798875231391 (eBook PDF)

Image Credits: Getty: Jose Luis Pelaez Inc/DigitalVision, 28–29; iStock: Denisfilm, 14, Dobrila Vignjevic, 27, fstop123, 15, PeopleImages, 1, 7, RuslanDashinsky, 10, Sadeugra, 11, 32; Shutterstock: Astakhin Evgeny, 20, Bohdan Malitskiy, 2–3, FrentaN, 26, GOLFX, 22–23, Jim Cumming, 24–25, New Africa, 6, OGI75, 30–31, Pikovit, 8–9, 12–13, 16–17, Pixel-Shot, cover, Shawn Hamilton, 21, SvetaZi, 18–19, TY Lim, 4–5

Printed and bound in China. 6274